Original title:
Weeds of Wonder

Copyright © 2025 Creative Arts Management OÜ
All rights reserved.

Author: Elliot Harrison
ISBN HARDBACK: 978-1-80566-689-9
ISBN PAPERBACK: 978-1-80566-974-6

Wandering Buds of the Backlot

In the cracks of concrete, they thrive,
A motley crew, so jive alive.
With colors bright, they steal the scene,
In the tall grass, they dance like queens.

Bumblebees chuckle, they buzz along,
To a tune that's quirky, a silly song.
With roots like mischief, they take their stand,
A circus of petals, oh so unplanned.

The Lament of Ignored Blooms

In the corner, they sigh and pout,
Longing for sunshine, craving clout.
With their heads held low, a tragic show,
Oh, how they wish for a garden glow!

But a wayward cat naps on their bed,
With dreams of fish swimming in his head.
While hapless blooms want a glance or two,
They just get brushed off like old, worn glue.

Serendipitous Growth in Unlikely Places

A crack in the pavement, a sign of glee,
A sprout peeks up like, 'Look at me!'
With little hearts made of whimsy and cheer,
They giggle at life; nonsense is near.

Who knew a sidewalk could be so bright?
They host little parties in the dead of night.
Wobbling like drunks, they sway to the tune,
Rocking their petals under the moon.

Floral Rebels in the Sunlight

They wear their colors loud and bold,
Rebelling against the norms of old.
With roots in the soil and dreams in the sky,
They laugh at the pruners who pass them by.

These floral tricksters, cheeky and spry,
They throw a fiesta as the world goes by.
In garden beds or a forgotten lane,
They blossom with joy, oh sweet disdain!

Tales of Life from the Unknown

In a garden full of chaos, you'll find,
Sneaky critters plotting, oh so unkind.
A dandelion winks, oh what a prank!
With petals like sun, it's the king of the bank.

A runaway lettuce, beneath a pie pan,
Hiding from rabbits, best-laid plans ran.
Tomatoes in sneakers, they laugh and they race,
While zucchini dance, claiming their space.

Bounties of the Unpruned

In corners untouched, the treasures reside,
Surprise melons giggle, with nowhere to hide.
Radishes tumbling like silly old fools,
In a land of misfits, they stand with the rules.

Cherries all blushing, they won't be ignored,
While mushrooms play hide and seek with the hoard.
The beans cozy up, all tangled and snug,
In the party of plants, they give a warm hug.

The Grace of Wayward Growth

Oh look at the celery, so stubborn and tall,
It sways with the breeze, taking heed of the call.
Cucumbers gossip, wrapped round the fence,
With tales of their travels — oh what a suspense!

Chives in a fedora, acting so suave,
Trying to woo herbs, with their irresistible charm.
Garlic in sunglasses, so cool and aloof,
Together they bicker, but all in good proof.

Dreams Sprouting Through the Cracks

Out of the sidewalk, a sprout braves the day,
With aspirations so bold, it finds its own way.
A hen in the yard clucks loud with delight,
As she watches the dreams bloom from morning till night.

In the shadow of bricks, a wildflower smiles,
Packing up hopes for the journey of miles.
Though fate may be fickle, with twists and with turns,
In laughter and joy, the spirit still yearns.

The Language of Dandelions

In fields where yellow giggles sway,
They dance and twirl, a bright display.
With fluffy heads, they blow and tease,
Whispers of mischief in the breeze.

They say, 'Oh, pluck me if you dare!'
But roots run deep, they know how to care.
A game of hide-and-seek they play,
As children chase their dreams away.

Their laughter fills the summer air,
In every nook and cranny, bare.
A kingdom wild, a sprightly scene,
Where every patch is gaily green.

So raise a toast to yellow cheer,
To every sprout that dares appear.
For in their mischief, life unfolds,
In tales of wonders yet untold.

Time in the Thicket

In tangled vines and patches tall,
A comedy of growth enthralls.
The rabbits giggle as they munch,
On leafy snacks, their favorite lunch.

A sprout pops up, then hides away,
'Not yet!' it sings, 'Let's play all day!'
Among the plucky, playful greens,
A carnival of funny scenes.

The thicket winks with secret charms,
A world of chaos, hugs, and balms.
Each twist and turn, a surprise awaits,
Where laughter blooms and fun creates.

So come and frolic in the shade,
Where whimsy's woven, fun displayed.
For in this growth, the jesters play,
In every cheer, a wild bouquet.

Ephemeral Whispers of Untamed Growth

A tumble of greens, a merry show,
Where secrets sprout and soft winds blow.
Each blade a joke, each bud a pun,
In nature's humor, we find our fun.

With petals popping like party hats,
Daring critters chase the chitchats.
The hummingbirds join in the feast,
On laughter's nectar, they never cease.

A patch of chaos, wild and free,
Is where the heart finds glee, you see.
With every bloom, a smile born,
In the laughter of the lush, we're sworn.

So dance among the greens so bright,
In their funny whispers, find delight.
For in each sprout, a tale takes flight,
In untamed joy, our spirits ignite.

Echoes of Forgotten Seeds

In the garden, chaos reigns,
A cabbage whispers jokes,
While carrots wear their funny hats,
And broccoli sings in cloaks.

Lettuce hides behind the fence,
Telling tales of silly pranks,
Tomatoes rolling on the ground,
Plotting secrets, laughing ranks.

Radishes, in costumes bright,
Have staged a merry play,
While onions giggle in the dusk,
They're tears of laughter, hey!

So come and join this leafy crew,
Where every sprout's a clown,
In a world where antics bloom,
And silliness wears a crown.

The Artistry of Unwanted Growth

In the garden, weeds take pride,
With a waltz beneath the sun,
Dandelions throwing parties,
While snails join in the fun.

They twirl amidst neglected beds,
Performing with such flair,
The daisies roll their eyes, annoyed,
At all the ruckus there.

But hidden in this messy plot,
Are talents yet unseen,
A patch of clover tap-dancing,
In a riotous routine.

So let them grow, these rebels bold,
In nature's wild ballet,
For in their chaos, laughter blooms,
And joy finds its own way.

Tales from the Edge of the Garden

At the edge, a tale unfolds,
Where quirky sprouts abide,
Squash plants planning mischief loud,
With radishes as their guide.

Petunias swear they saw them sneak,
To the neighbor's flower bed,
A plot to 'borrow' sunbeams bright,
To paint their leafy spread.

Cucumbers giggle, twist, and turn,
In a fumbled chase for light,
While bell peppers discuss their dreams,
Of being stars one night.

Oh, the stories whispered soft,
Among the roots, and dew,
Where every plant has something wild,
And sneaky tales come true.

Harmonies of the Unruly Sprouts

In a patch of vibrant hues,
The sprouts begin to sing,
As cabbage strums a ukulele,
And beets play tambourine.

A sunflower leads the choir bright,
With sunbeams in its hair,
While kale joins in, all full of zest,
In a funk-inspired flair.

The peas hop in with playful steps,
Dancing through the plot,
And every turn brings laughter loud,
In this garden, oh so hot.

So turn your ears to nature's tunes,
Where chaos finds its flow,
For in the laughter of the green,
We find a joyful show.

Fragrant Fables of the Uninvited

In gardens where the daisies play,
A broccoli dreams of a Broadway sway.
With carrots critiquing their leafy plight,
They giggle and wriggle 'neath the moonlight.

A daffodil donned a flamboyant hat,
While a dandelion flirted with a cat.
The parsley whispered secrets so sweet,
As the turnips tapped their tiny feet.

A Symphony in Overgrown Fields

The trumpet vine sings the loudest tune,
While clovers hop like an afternoon.
A corn cob conductor waves his stick,
As the grasshoppers jump in a rhythmic flick.

With every note, the thistles prance,
Inviting the ladybugs to dance.
Their laughter spreads far as the crickets chirp,
In this grassy paradise, no need for a burp.

Rooted Mysteries of the Uncultivated

In the brush, where secrets lie,
A rogue onion dreams of a pie.
It plots and it schemes, with garlic bold,
To roast in the oven—a treasure to hold.

The radishes tell old tales of misleads,
Of epic quests through forgotten seeds.
They chuckle and snicker, all snug underground,
Where mysteries brew all around.

The Dance of the Wayward Petals

Petals twirl in a cheerful swirl,
As the wind gives their colors a whirl.
A butterfly, dressed in jewels and gold,
Whispers sweet nothings, so bold yet so cold.

In a ballet of blooms, the roses tease,
While violets giggle at dandelion breeze.
A cheerful chaos in the sun's warm glow,
The garden's a stage for the flora to show.

The Poetry of Unruly Growth

In cracks of the sidewalk, they bravely sprout,
Waving their arms like they're dancing about.
With hats made of mud and shoes of grass,
They throw a wild party, no need to pass.

Their petals are laughing, the colors are bright,
In a world that insists they should be out of sight.
They play peek-a-boo in the garden of strife,
Claiming their space, full of vigor and life.

These little green rascals, with roots that insist,
Are laughing at rules, making grown-ups twist.
They twirl in the breeze, oblivious and bold,
In their quirky parade, the fun must unfold.

So here's to the mischief, to growth that defies,
Those uninvited guests under bright, sunny skies.
For in every odd patch, there's a story to tell,
Of nature's own jesters, who bid us farewell.

Wild Wonders Among Pedestrians

In between the bricks on the bustling street,
They pop up like clowns, with surprising flair and heat.
With a wink and a giggle, they wave at the passers,
In this concrete jungle, they're the true masters.

They jive with the pigeons, they chat with the bees,
Spilling their secrets along with the trees.
Oh, what a sight, as they chaotically dance,
In their own little world, they don't need your chance.

Among heels and sneakers, with roots snug and tight,
They boast their weirdness, it's a wonderful sight.
The commuters walk past, heads down on their phones,
While blossoms sip coffee, exchanging their tones.

Here's to the flowers that thrive in the cracks,
Who refuse to conform, who don't follow tracks.
In this urban delight, they sing songs all day,
Creating a laughter in their peculiar way.

Genesis of the Uninvited

In the corners of gardens, they plan their takeover,
With roots all a-tangle, and blooms with a favor.
Oh, how they giggle, with joy they expand,
A party of nature, just not what we planned.

They crash all the picnics, with colors so wild,
Throwing a ruckus as if they were a child.
With invitations lost, they still find a way,
To liven the space on a dull summer day.

Like confetti from heaven, they scatter so free,
In patches of sunlight, they jump with glee.
With a hearty cheer, the sprouts take the stage,
In this unruly dance, they laugh at the cage.

So here's to the rascals who live their own lore,
Taking life by storm, always wanting more.
Genuine jesters with jubilant might,
Celebrate their existence, under stars so bright.

Cosmic Play in the Ferns

In the gloomy shadows, they swirl and unfold,
Dressed in the emerald, with secrets to hold.
Little fronds frolic beneath the tall trees,
With a giggle and wiggle, they sway in the breeze.

Like a stand-up act, they tease with a twist,
Knocking over mushrooms, they can't be dismissed.
In their leafy embrace, they share a good jest,
Who knew that the ferns would be nature's best guest?

They poke fun at the daisies for being so plain,
While winking at daisies, they dance in the rain.
With laughter as soft as the dew in the morn,
These cozy green pranksters leave all feeling warm.

A universe buzzing with giggles and cheer,
In the quietest corners, their antics appear.
So next time you wander in forest designs,
Look closely for laughter where nature aligns.

Celestial Visions in the Untended Earth

In gardens where no rules apply,
A dandelion wears a crown on high.
Buttercups shout with colors so bright,
While sunflowers giggle, chasing the light.

A rogue spinach dreams of being a star,
While rogue radishes plot from afar.
With roots that dance and leaves that prance,
They throw the strict weeds out of their chance.

Blooms of the Undeserved Canvas.

In patches where chaos starts to grow,
Petunias laugh at what we think we know.
Lilies gossip about the next big trend,
As daisies scheme to find a new friend.

Forget the order, here's a funny mess,
Cats sit amused at nature's dress.
Who knew the soil would play such a role,
In turning a weed into heart and soul?

Wild Blossoms of Curiosity

A thistle queen wears a dress of green,
Her spiky crown, a royal sheen.
Chickweed sips from a raindrop's gleam,
While clovers conspire, forming a team.

With petals that prank and colors that sway,
They plot their takeover in a cheeky way.
What's planned is unruly, what's seen is a riot,
These blooms let loose, the garden's a riot.

Untamed Dreams in the Cracks

Amidst the pavement, a smile breaks free,
A sprout with a vision, quite bold and carefree.
Concrete don't scare, it starts a parade,
As laughter and petals make quite the charade.

In the tiniest spaces, the fun's just begun,
With wild ambitions, they dance in the sun.
Nature's mischief finds home in the grime,
Transforming the mundane into something sublime.

The Secret Lives of Unsought Blossoms

In a garden where laughter grows,
The daisies plot in comical prose.
They dance on the breeze, a silly parade,
Whispering secrets in sunlight's cascade.

Petunias gossip, their petals ablaze,
While tulips are off in their whimsical ways.
A rogue sunflower twirls, what a sight!
Chasing after bumblebees with pure delight.

Each hidden sprout holds a tale of its own,
Of love in the soil, of seeds that have flown.
With worms as their audience, roots stir and tease,
Sprouting laughter beneath the tall trees.

Though overlooked, they twinkle and beam,
In nature's madcap, they stifle a scream.
With petals of joy in the most silly hues,
These unsought blossoms share their furry muse.

Radiance in the Rough

Amidst the cracks, they stretch and peek,
With tattered hats, these sprigs are chic.
Their vibrant cheer wraps the gray,
Like clowns in the garden, they steal the day.

A dandelion spouts a giggly tune,
While thistles spin tales 'neath the moon.
They don't care what others think,
Just thriving and vibing, they wink and blink.

Creating ruckus in dignified lawns,
With antics that stretch from dusk to dawn.
They rebel with flair and a hint of glee,
Painting the world with a wild decree.

Oh, look how they flourish, defiant and bold,
In patches of chaos—don't do what you're told.
They bask in the wild, their laughter is tough,
These gems in the dirt shine bright in the rough.

Mysterious Vines of the Wayward Land

In corners forgotten, the vines intertwine,
With tales of mischief and grapes from fine wine.
They wiggle and jiggle on trellises old,
Whispering secrets too cheeky to hold.

Adventurous shoots take paths of their own,
Climbing up fences, they've overgrown.
A snicker escapes from the tangled spread,
As they tickle the toes of all those who tread.

They wear hats of leaves and shades of delight,
Entangling the world, they step into light.
With a giggle of fruit at the end of the way,
They dangle like jests in the heat of the day.

Oh, how they flourish with style so divine,
Making mischief, those vines just recline.
In a world that forgot how to play and roam,
These mysterious strands have carved their own home.

Chronicles of the Untamed Blooms

From cracks in the sidewalk, they burst with flair,
　Telling stories of growth with audacious care.
　In unexpected places, their laughter ignites,
　Crafting legends by day and by chilly nights.

　The raggedy roses boast colors so wild,
　While violets giggle, bringing joy like a child.
　With petals like capes, they fly through the air,
　　Creating a ruckus, without a single care.

In thickets and edges where no one would check,
　The untamed blooms plot with a touch of respect.
　For in every crack, they see a broad stage,
　Where nature's odd actors perform a fun page.

　So raise up a cheer for the misfits of green,
With winks and with quirks, they paint the unseen.
　They may not fit in, but they shine with a hue,
These chroniclers bold share a world that's brand new.

Resilient Whispers of the Unkempt

In the garden, laughter thrives,
Uninvited guests, the cheeky hives.
They sprout in colors, wild and bright,
With mischief that brings pure delight.

Oh, the dandelions dance with glee,
Spreading fluff like a jester's spree.
While neighbors fret and pull them out,
These merry greens just laugh and shout.

With roots that clutch and wink so sly,
They claim the ground, oh my, oh my!
Embracing chaos, they proudly sway,
In a land where order's just passé.

So raise a toast to the plants that rule,
With laughter as their golden fuel.
For in the mess, joy finds its way,
Unkempt whispers make the day play.

Hidden Gardens of Imagination

In secret spots where weird things grow,
A pineapple's hat, a broccoli's bow.
Carrots that giggle, tomatoes that sing,
In this land, all oddities take wing.

Mischief blooms in shades of pink,
While radishes wink and wink.
With each new sprout, a tale unfolds,
As lettuce heroes break the molds.

The scarecrow tells the funniest jokes,
His friends are quirky, giggly folks.
Frolicsome ferns and smart aleck beans,
In this garden of dreams, nothing's as it seems.

When raindrops fall, they tapdance around,
In puddles, their joy is easily found.
So let your thoughts wander and roam,
In this vibrant patch, you're always at home.

Fragile Fortitude in the Unruly

Oh, fragile blooms in tattered dresses,
Claim the garden with bold caresses.
They stumble, trip, then laugh out loud,
In their chaos, they're fiercely proud.

A sunflower stands, tall and spry,
Wobbling under a squirrel's sly.
Showing grit in the wildest ways,
Who needs order on sunny days?

The violets giggle in the wind's embrace,
Falling over, but never losing grace.
With roots so deep and hearts so free,
In their unruly dance, they find glee.

So let them twirl, let them play,
In every wild and crazy way.
For in their haphazard, joyful plot,
Lies the magic that can't be bought.

Serendipity Among the Thorns

In bramble patches, surprises bloom,
Cactus friendships spark in the gloom.
With prickly hugs and sweet little smiles,
Even thorns can go the extra miles.

Butterflies tease, flitting about,
In the thickets where giggles sprout.
Here hidden treasures are often found,
With whispers of joy, echoing around.

A rogue vine climbs with boisterous flair,
Around the gate, it swings without a care.
With every twist, it tells a new tale,
Of unlikely friendships that set sail.

So dance with joy, in joyful embrace,
Among the thorns, find your own place.
For serendipity thrives in the wild,
Teaching us life can be goofy and mild.

Harmonies of the Uncontrolled

In a garden that's a little wild,
The dandelions dance and smile.
They sprout like jokes, quite out of hand,
Making chaos in the land.

Clover giggles as it grows,
Tickling toes with its fuzzy toes.
They sing a song that's loud and bold,
In gardens where the tales are told.

Journeys Through the Wild Underbrush

Through the thicket, off we roam,
Finding treasures far from home.
A thistle waves like a flag on high,
While butterflies laugh and fly.

Beneath the brambles, secrets hide,
Where nature's quirks take us for a ride.
A vine swings low, just like a tease,
You think it's a pet, but it's just a sneeze!

Revelations in Nature's Chaos

In the balmy air, mischief brews,
A tangle of greens in zany hues.
With every sprout, a giggle springs,
As frogs join in and the jester sings.

The rules of gardens start to bend,
As the unruly plants make a friend.
One unruly branch, with leaves so spry,
Whispers secrets that make us sigh.

The Splendor of the Untamed

Here lies a patch of pure delight,
Where every bloom looks bold and bright.
The sunflowers wear their goofy grins,
While nature's party just begins.

A wild thyme waltz in breezy air,
Bouncing about without a care.
With every twist and every spin,
The laughter of green is where we begin.

Secrets Beneath the Soil

In the garden, roots all twist,
Hidden antics, can't resist.
Bunnies laugh, they dance and swirl,
While worms insist on digging, girl!

Underneath, a party thrives,
Moles wear hats, they're all alive.
Grubs recite their favorite lines,
And beetles toast with juicy vines.

Ants debate in well-dressed suits,
Who will win the dance-off hoots?
With tickled petals and roots so bold,
The secret lives are tales untold.

When sun creeps in, they freeze in fright,
Pretend to sleep, it's quite a sight.
Yet come the moon, they all awake,
To jig and jive, for laughter's sake.

Unruly Beauty of the Unseen

In shadows lies a cheerful crew,
With dandelion wigs, they blew.
Ladybugs in polka dots,
Tease the snails, they're such good sorts.

Tall grass tickles tiny feet,
As baby toads attempt to beat.
A wiggly worm starts breakdancing,
Uncontrolled fun, is that romancing?

Fireflies spark, they share bright dreams,
While rabbits plot their silly schemes.
A rogue potato swears it's fleet,
Dressed in dirt, it's quite the treat.

The chaos blooms in every patch,
Where nature's whimsy meets a catch.
Amongst the roots and leafy things,
Laughter sprouts while freedom sings.

Nature's Forgotten Jewels

Amid the muck, so rich and bold,
Lie treasures waiting to be told.
A rusty nail dons emerald green,
While tiny flowers burst the scene.

Each pebble hides a secret charm,
A ladybug with tiny arms.
They gather round for tea so fine,
On porcelain leaves, they sip and dine.

Reclining 'neath an old oak's shade,
A peculiar pact is surely made.
Singing frogs with crowns of grass,
Declare a royal dance en masse.

Disguised as dirt, they laughed and twirled,\nThese gems
of life, so unexplored.
In every root, in every nook,
Nature's laughter's in every book.

Echoes of Unfurling Leaves

Leaves giggle as they spread so wide,
Telling tales the breezes guide.
A grasshopper croaks a feathery song,
While petals clap, all swaying along.

Each bud blooms with a secret cheer,
Whispers of joy when friends are near.
A butterfly's wig twirls in delight,
Spreading color from morning to night.

Vines weave stories through tangled mess,
In perfect chaos, they find success.
Singing softly to the hum of bees,
They dance in time with playful breeze.

The forest floor, a stage so bright,
Guides all things to join the light.
With every rustle, laughter reigns,
In nature's play, there are no chains.

Fleeting Moments in the Patch

In the garden, something stirs,
A dandelion wearing spurs.
With a wink, it starts to prance,
Inviting all to join the dance.

A ladybug starts to slide,
On a leaf, it tries to hide.
But a curious cat swings by,
And gives a startled little cry.

A beetle boasts of silver sheen,
While a flower wears a green machine.
They trade their secrets, oh what fun,
In a world where laughter's spun.

So next time you stroll through the green,
Look closely, and you'll surely glean.
The joy of nature's silly show,
In every nook where wild things grow.

Marvels of Nature's Recklessness

A sprout pokes through the morning dew,
With orange socks and a bright pink shoe.
It shouts, 'Look at me, I'm quite the sight!'
As hummingbirds buzz with sheer delight.

A sunflower wears a crooked crown,
Wobbling proudly in its gown.
While ants march in a perfect line,
Thinking they're on a grand design.

A mushroom dons a polka-dot hat,
Saying, 'Oh, look at me, I'm rather fat!'
It gives a wink, and the bugs all cheer,
For daring to dress so without fear.

As clouds drift lazily in the sky,
Nature giggles with a hearty sigh.
For in this realm of quirky glee,
There's always a twist in what you see.

A Symphony of Untamed Growth

In a patch, where chaos reigns,
A saxophone plays in wild lanes.
The weeds all dance, oh what a sight,
With roots so tangled, they feel just right.

The daisies hum their joyful tune,
While crickets tap dance under the moon.
A dandelion bursts into song,
With off-key notes that carry so strong.

A thistle croons with spiky flair,
While butterflies swirl, not a single care.
They twirl and swirl in nature's ball,
With laughter echoing through it all.

So join the jam in the garden fair,
Where wild things sing without a care.
In nature's choir, you'll find the cheer,
And funny notes that bring you near.

The Dance of Nature's Oddities

A twig declares it's now a pole,
Getting ready for a dance console.
The flowers giggle as they sway,
Best buddies joining in the play.

A snail wears shades, it's quite the star,
Slicking back its tiny hair from afar.
It strikes a pose, then starts to crawl,
Calling the garden to the grand ball.

Grasshoppers leap with flair and zest,
Challenging the squirrel, 'Who's the best?'
But the squirrel just rolls in the dirt,
Chasing crumbs, simple and alert.

The sun dips low, the shadows grow,
Yet laughter echoes in the glow.
When nature's quirks come out to play,
You'll find the magic leads the way.

Idiosyncrasies in Green Slumber

In a garden full of quirks,
Plants wear socks and dance with smirks.
Caterpillars spin their tales,
While dandelions plan grand scales.

A rogue tomato rolls on by,
With tiny arms, it waves goodbye.
Radishes don party hats,
As ladybugs shake their chitchat.

The leafy greens play hide and seek,
With roots that giggle, oh so cheek!
A carrot twirls, quite in a sprawl,
While mushrooms share the latest call.

In this patch, we laugh and play,
With all the oddities on display.
Beneath the sun, they're free to roam,
Embracing every quirky gnome.

Colorful Mischief of Nature's Hands

A sunflower dons a silly grin,
As breezes tease the leaves akin.
Purple beans run round the way,
In this carnival of wild display.

The peas have hats, quite snug and neat,
And wink at carrots, oh so sweet.
Strawberries slide on slippery dew,
While rhubarbs cheer, 'What shall we do?'

Bees buzz around like playful sprites,
In a ruckus of polka dot flights.
Nature's mischief's bright and bold,
A circus of colors to behold.

So join the fun in this rich realm,
Where chaos reigns, and joys overwhelm.
In every sprout, a chance to play,
In the garden's dance, we'll sway away.

Mending the Fabric of Untamed Beauty

With threads of green, they stitch a tale,
Of dancing leaves that laugh and wail.
A patchwork quilt of blooms and scents,
In this wild realm, no need for tents.

Grasshopper's leaps, a comic act,
While roots entwine with a cheerful pact.
Squirrels sporting coats of fluff,
Claim the title, 'Nature's Tough'.

The wildflowers spill colors bright,
As they twirl in the morning light.
A festoon of fragrance fills the air,
Nature's laughter joins in the flair.

So let us weave this joyous spree,
In every crease, a mystery.
Embrace the madness of it all,
In nature's fabric, we shall fall.

Fractals of Uncultured Splendor

In the garden's playful mess,
We find humor in nature's dress.
Daisies wear shoes two sizes too big,
While hedgehogs waltz in a whimsical jig.

The ferns quietly plot their rave,
While grass peeks out from every cave.
The flowers giggle, swapping tales,
Of mishaps involving bees and snails.

Wild pumpkins practice their stand-up,
Joking toads flick their tiny cups.
Collards boast of their leafy games,
As vines tangle in love's sweet claims.

So frolic through this verdant play,
Where merry chaos leads the way.
In each odd sprout, we find delight,
In the fractals of a green-lit night.

The Unruly Chorus of Fields

In gardens ripe with chaos grown,
A dance of greens that won't be sown.
They jive and wiggle in the breeze,
Declaring war on roses' ease.

With roots that laugh and leave a mess,
They wear their wildness like a dress.
A chorus of vines and blooms combine,
In this turf where sun does shine.

Each petal prances, each leaf twirls,
As butterflies perform their whirls.
Amid the beauties, bold they stand,
These joyful rascals, unplanned.

The sun shines down on green-haired jest,
Who needs a map? It's all a quest!
Look closely, and you might just find,
A giggling patch, a giggling kind.

Rhapsody in the Unwanted Patch

A symphony of unexpected sights,
Outlaws decked in nature's flights.
They hum a tune of pure delight,
In shades of green, from morn to night.

Where daisies fear to wear their crowns,
These sprightly invaders dance in gowns.
With antics bold, they steal the show,
And revel in their wild glow.

In tangled beds where none should dwell,
They ring the laughter's joyful bell.
While gardeners sigh, these rebels cheer,
Turning frowns to grins all year.

Their melodies spread, both loud and clear,
Testing patience, but we hold dear.
We can't help but laugh, bemused,
At nature's scheme, artfully confused.

Quirks of Nature's Palette

In every cranny where they sprout,
There's a dash of fun beyond the clout.
They twist and shout with leafy flair,
Painting laughter in the fresh air.

A patchwork quilt of odd design,
Each bloom a joke, while roots entwine.
Their games can turn a solemn place,
Into a party full of grace.

With colors bright, they wave hello,
As bees and ants join in the show.
From blushing reds to goofy greens,
They stir up joy in nature's scenes.

So let them thrive, these funny sprouts,
In every nook where laughter shouts.
Their quirkiness, a heart's delight,
In every garden, wrong or right.

A Voyage Through Tangled Paths

Upon the winding trails we roam,
Where laughter hides in every loam.
These cheery chaps, with roots unbound,
Are found in every furrowed ground.

With mischief brewing in the sun,
They hold a party, just for fun!
A detour here might lead to glee,
As they conspire with the bumblebee.

In fields where neatness takes a flight,
They celebrate their wild delight.
Each turn reveals a new surprise,
In a journey where laughter lies.

So stroll along their tangled trails,
Where silly antics never pales.
With every twist, there's joy anew,
On this hilarious ride, join too!

A Tapestry of Untamed Life

In corners of chaos, they dance and twirl,
Sneaky little sprigs in a chaotic whirl.
With laughter and giggles, they dodge the shears,
Waving their leaves, flinging out cheers.

They pop up with flair from cracks in the ground,
In patches of color, they play all around.
Dandelion dreams in a buttercup dress,
Making the garden a humorous mess.

With roots like a secret, they stretch far and wide,
Uninvited guests on a wild, bumpy ride.
Planting their flags, they claim every inch,
In a wee riot of greens, they make the world pinch.

Oh what an uproar, a botanical spree,
Tiny green rebels, as merry as can be.
With each little sprout, a chuckle ensues,
In the garden of giggles, there's no time to lose.

The Surprising Resilience of Green

Under the fence where the grass doesn't care,
Squabbling with daisies, they dance through the air.
They tumble and twist in a masquerade ball,
These riotous greens have the best time of all.

From sidewalk to pot, they simply invade,
With top hats of moss and a nature parade.
Giggling to sunshine, they shimmy and sway,
What's a little chaos in the light of the day?

They frolic with roots in an old garden chair,
Spreading their joy like a careless affair.
With humor in leaves, they chuckle and boast,
Making the world a curious toast.

Oh, who states "you can't" when they clearly know,
That the cheeky green squad has an ongoing show?
With whimsy and wit, they turn up with glee,
And life in the open is wild as can be.

Nature's Uninvited Guests

A party of colors in an ill-kept lot,
Unruly yet lively, they're tied in a knot.
From flowerbeds gleaming to sidewalks that hum,
These party-crashers won't dawdle or succumb!

Bursts of green laughter in the corners so tight,
They climb and they cling in the warm, golden light.
Comical figures that wiggle and sway,
Making grand plans for a wild garden play.

Cloaked in bright leaves with a penchant to tease,
Taking the garden down with every breeze.
They're nature's own jesters in a riotous bloom,
Turning a patch into a whimsical room.

So here's to the tricksters, the quirky and bold,
Who thrive on the laughter and chase off the cold.
With giggles and cheer, they make nature a jest,
Proving that chaos can sometimes be best.

Innocence in the Overgrowth

Amidst the tall grasses, mischief unfolds,
Where laughs float like petals, and humor takes hold.
Tiny green critters with cheeky delight,
Giggle as day turns to whimsical night.

They sneak out to play where no one can see,
In shadows of roots, they dance wild and free.
With innocence twinkling from every green shoot,
A story of joy in a muddled-up route.

With dandelion wishes and clovers that cheer,
They tickle the hearts, drawing smiles near.
In a tapestry woven of innocence pure,
The laughter of green lends a magical lure.

So let's celebrate sprigs that burst from the ground,
In the laughter of chaos, a delight to be found.
With every small growth, there's a chance to unveil,
The silly side of nature that's bound to prevail.

Unraveled Mysteries of the Wilderness

In the garden, a sage was found,
Chasing shadows, spinning round.
With dandelions in a hat so bright,
Laughing at squirrels, what a sight!

An old cactus danced near the gate,
Shimmied and shook, it felt so great.
Beneath the lawn, a secret crew,
Of gnomes and toads, plotting too.

A flower's voice rose like a thrill,
Telling stories of space and chill.
Bright roses giggled with delight,
As bees played jazz under moonlight.

When the rain poured down, hats took a flight,
The sun peeked out, what a sunny sight!
Every leaf was a cap or a shoe,
In the wilderness, so much to do!

Wanderlust Among Stubborn Shoots

Little sprouts stand, proud and tall,
Filling the garden with a curious call.
They planned a trip, no map in hand,
To other gardens, so vastly grand.

With whispers of dreams, they took to the skies,
Chasing butterflies, laughing with sighs.
A daisy wore shades, so debonair,
While a tulip sprawled, without a care.

In their way, a snail took a stroll,
Claiming the path, playing its role.
They spun and twirled, oh what a show!
Zipping past weeds, oh how they'd grow!

When nighttime fell, they gathered near,
Sharing tales, full of cheer.
Among stubborn shoots, adventures unfold,
Every little moment, a treasure untold!

The Wild Craft of Possibility

In a patch where no one would dare to tread,
Sprouted fancies, both green and red.
A tangle of dreams, so unexpected,
Danced in the breeze, joyfully connected.

A quirky flower wore mismatched socks,
While his buddy laughed, juggling rocks.
They planned a festival—oh what a blast,
A carnival of colors from future and past!

Among them, a weed with a curious grin,
Told tales of treasure buried within.
With cheeky charm, it spun a web,
Of laughter and mischief, how they'd ebb!

At dusk, they twirled beneath the stars,
While crickets played tunes on old guitars.
In wild craft, they found their home,
In paths of chance, forever to roam!

Enchantment in Each Forgotten Stem

Beneath the leaves, a party ensued,
A wild affair with joy imbued.
Forget-me-nots rocking tiny hats,
Sipping dew tea and chatting with cats.

The sun was a jester, cracking jokes,
While shadows joined in with playful strokes.
Each forgotten stem, a story to share,
Of magic and laughter, suspended in air.

A rogue dandelion spun in a whirl,
In a tutu of fluff, oh what a girl!
She taught the tulips to dance and sway,
As the moon peeked out, lighting their play.

When morning came, they all took a bow,
In the garden of dreams, oh how they'd vow!
For enchantment lives in every bloom,
A funny tale woven in nature's loom!

Nature's Hidden Whimsy

In a patch of green, they sprout and dance,
With leaves that wiggle, they take their chance.
Tickling toes as you walk by,
These cheeky green things catch the eye.

Buds with colors that clash and fight,
Flaunting their styles like stars at night.
Who knew the ground could throw such a show?
A riot of laughter where wild things grow.

With pots and pans, they raise a cheer,
Mischief blooms, far and near.
Fleeting giggles in the garden's heart,
With each little sprout, a whimsical art.

So tiptoe through, enjoy the jest,
In the wild where nonsense is best.
Amongst the serious, they play and twirl,
Nature's jesters in a joyful swirl.

Unruly Blossoms at Dusk

As twilight falls, oh what a sight,
Floofy flowers prepare for flight.
With petals flailing, they start to bloom,
Filling the night with a sweet perfume.

They giggle in colors, bold and bright,
Creating chaos, what a delight!
In a frolicsome brawl, they twist and spin,
Messy bouquets that never keep in.

From pots to pathways, they spread their grace,
Inviting bumbles to join their race.
A party forms under the darkening skies,
As bees and bugs hold their quirky ties.

With laughter echoing through the leaves,
They toast to the night, like carefree thieves.
So come, report for nature's own fun,
Where unruly blooms greet the setting sun.

The Beauty Beneath the Thorns

In a tangle of thorns, a surprise awaits,
Secretive sprigs test their fates.
Daring to poke through, sly and spry,
Crafting a play where the brave can fly.

Little chaps in green, wrapped with pride,
Hiding from Bulldogs just outside.
With their hearts all aglow and staggering charm,
They blend in the chaos, spreading warm.

Every prick tells a cheeky tale,
Of winsome blooms that refuse to fail.
With laughter and joy, they flourish untamed,
Beauty in chaos, eternally unclaimed.

So tip back your hats and applaud this crew,
For in the wild, possibilities brew.
Amidst the thorns, a party's begun,
Beneath the fierce, there's always fun.

Secrets of the Untamed Garden

In the garden of secrets, giggles grow,
With plants that plot and play just for show.
Snickering leaves whisper tall tales,
As nightly critters ride on their trails.

Petals that chatter, boasting their flair,
Daring the world with a cheeky dare.
Swinging the evening with colors so wild,
Each bloom, a riddle, nature's own child.

Among the chaos where laughter thrives,
Bumblebees bounce, while the mischief arrives.
Planting their jokes in the soft twilight,
Unraveled wonders take cheerful flight.

So dig into life, let the madness begin,
Find joy in the secrets, dance in each spin.
For amidst the wild, a jester's parade,
In the untamed garden, our joy's displayed.

Enchanted Flora of the Forgotten Path

In a garden where socks tend to roam,
Grew an army of flowers that call it home.
Each petal wears stripes, a real fashion show,
Swaying and dancing, they steal the show.

The daisies form bands, with roots made of brass,
Playing sweet tunes on the soft green grass.
While the tulips wear hats, all crooked and bright,
An oddball parade, a charming delight!

Amongst bricks and stones, they stubbornly poke,
Sharing their secrets, or just having a joke.
With laughter and giggles, the weeds spin a tale,
Of growth through the cracks, they shall never fail.

So if you wander down that forgotten old path,
Expect a surprise; laughter follows their math.
For in that wild patch where the lost things thrive,
Flora of fancy keeps the spirit alive.

Resilient Green Hearts

In cracks and crevices, they sprout with glee,
Chasing the sun, as happy as can be.
Blades of mystique, with roots like a dance,
Freestyle existence, they prance and prance.

With a wink to the daisies, they're never quite shy,
Sporting their colors, oh, me oh my!
Each leaf a little joke, each stem a tall tale,
With a giggle of green, they'll never derail.

Casting shadows where no one believes,
Twisting and twirling like playful thieves.
They laugh with the breezes, they tickle the skies,
In this jungle of jests, life's a big surprise.

So raise a toast to the humor they bring,
With each dandelion puff, we smile and sing.
These resilient hearts thrive, no need to amend,
In the garden of goof, they don't follow trends.

The Misfit's Bloom

In a forgotten corner where old tires rest,
Grew a flower that never knew it was blessed.
With petals that spiral, and colors askew,
This misfit's life, a whimsical view.

It wore shoes on its leaves and a hat made of straw,
Telling tall tales of the garden's big law.
A party of oddballs all gathered around,
For laughter and joy were eternally found.

While the roses rolled eyes, too proper to stay,
The misfit found joy in its bumpy ballet.
Each bloom a riot, each stem a wild ride,
In a world that neglected, it blossomed with pride.

So here's to the flowers who don't fit the mold,
In the garden of life, their stories unfold.
With a wink and a dance, they teach us to cheer,
For the quirky and odd are the ones we hold dear.

Wild Whispers in the Tall Grass

In the tall grass where secrets abound,
The whispers of nature create quite a sound.
With a chuckle and grin, the wild ones convene,
A riot of green in a grand, grassy scene.

"Did you see that cloud? It's a chicken!" they tease,
While rolling in laughter and dancing with ease.
Each blade of the grass shares a joke or a quirk,
From the mischief of rabbits to ants at their work.

They throw wild parties without any fuss,
Hosting bugs and birds, a jolly big plus.
With a tickle of wind, they all come alive,
In a world so mundane, they help us survive.

So if you should wander where the wild things collect,
Stop for a moment, share a giggle, reflect.
For the whispers of life in that tall, swaying mass,
Are a joyful reminder that we all can surpass.

Radiance in the Untamed Corners

In the cracks, the smiles bloom wide,
Dancing brown leaves with nothing to hide.
When grass disguises what we call neat,
It's a wild party beneath our feet.

Tiny flowers in a racing spree,
Waving their hands like they're wild and free.
With each gust, they twirl and spin,
Charming the lizards to join in the din.

Beneath the sky, they wiggle and sway,
Telling the soil, 'We are here to play!'
Cracks in the pavement hold secrets untold,
Of bravest little hearts brave and bold.

A patchwork quilt of misfit green,
Their joyful chaos is truly serene.
Laughter erupts as the flowers compete,
'The best party's here,' they shout with their beat.

The Charms of the Unwanted

In a garden that's neat, there's a comical sight,
A rogue sprout dancing, with all of its might.
'They call me a pest,' it shouts from the ground,
'But I'm here to show you how fun can be found!'

Rambunctious roots in a flower's fine dress,
Stir up the chaos with gleeful finesse.
'Toss me some sunlight, and watch me grow big!
While fancier blooms can only back jig.'

The daisies may giggle, the tulips may pout,
But the bold little sprout knows what it's about.
It sticks out its tongue, not a care to conform,
"Who needs your rules? I'll thrive in the storm!"

So let us embrace every wild little sprout,
In the patch of our garden, there's laughter throughout.
With every new bloom, our hearts will take flight,
For the charms of the unwanted, oh what a delight!

Flora of the Everyday Miracles

Amidst the concrete, there's treasure to find,
The everyday blooms are magic, unlined.
They giggle at traffic, and dance on the breeze,
Crafting a show just to make us all tease.

A dandelion's wish with its tiny white fluff,
Asking for dreams, oh it sure knows its stuff!
Children blow gently, spreading delight,
While grownups all frown, "It's a nuisance, alright!"

But deep in the roots of a thing we outcast,
Is joy wrapped in petals that bloom ever fast.
So let's stop to chuckle at nature's own call,
For the flora of miracles, we're here to enthrall.

Every green sprout holds a whimsical tale,
Of laughter in bloom as they seek to prevail.
In the busy of life, just slow down and see,
The joyful oddities, delightful and free.

Sweet Chaos Amongst the Greens

A jumbled patchwork, a garden of cheer,
Colors colliding, no tight fit here!
The grass has a party, the weeds all invite,
With daisies and daisies in a laugh-out-loud fright.

They gather 'round roots and share their wild songs,
With crickets on drums, they sing all day long.
Each creeping vine comes with silly dance moves,
Entwining in laughter, they all find their grooves.

Bees buzz in merriment, tickling the breeze,
While butterflies prance in the canopy trees.
Against all the odds, they weave a grand scene,
With chaos aplenty, sweet joy in between.

So here's to the ruckus, the bumbles, the blooms,
To nature's grand circus with all of its thrills.
In sweet chaos found where the wildflowers play,
A reminder we need: let laughter lead the way!

The Joy of Wild Abandon

In a garden where chaos grows,
The daisies dance in comical rows.
The carrots wear mismatched socks,
As laughter sprinkles, nature mocks.

Sunflowers chat with jolly glee,
While beetles buzz in harmony.
We embrace the wild, the strange, the bold,
With stories of silliness joyfully told.

Butterflies flaunt their fashion flair,
While rabbits hop without a care.
A squirrel juggles acorns high,
With giggles echoing through the sky.

Each twist and turn, a laugh awaits,
As nature plays, and joy creates.
In the insanity, we find our place,
In a world where fun leaves a trace.

Beauty in the Overlooked

A dandelion with a crooked grin,
Offers treasures hiding within.
A patch of clover without a plan,
Is where we find the funniest man.

The stones all sing a silly tune,
Beneath the lazy, lopsided moon.
With sleepy ants on a pizza quest,
In this odd garden, we feel our best.

A tumbleweed with a curtsy grand,
Prances round like a marching band.
With laughs erupting from plants galore,
They bind in joy forevermore.

Among the thorns, a rose does tease,
As bumblebees tickle with ease.
In the odd, we see the grace,
A beauty found in every place.

Whimsy Amongst the Grapplers

In tangled vines where giggles start,
A chubby gnome plays the saxophone art.
Tomatoes wear hats too big to hold,
While carrots argue about being bold.

The coy cucumbers sneak a peek,
At kale who humorously is meek.
Potatoes dance with floppy shoes,
In a game where nobody can lose.

Enthusiastic sprouts play tag in rows,
As sunbeams tickle their stubborn toes.
A playful breeze makes them swerve,
In this riotous dance, they find their verve.

Laughter echoes through the patch,
Each silly face a perfect match.
In those grapplers, the fun won't die,
It's whimsy here, so let's all fly!

Luminescence of the Undaunted

Bright mushrooms pop in neon shades,
　With goofy grins, they join parades.
Each one shines with courageous might,
　In the carnival of the moonlit night.

A sprightly fern leans with a sway,
　As crickets chirp in a cabaret.
Cheerful weeds give a playful bow,
　To forget-me-nots, who wonder how.

The bobbing leaves, like flapping wings,
　Are mockingly trying to be kings.
In this wild court, we laugh and cheer,
　For every oddity we hold dear.

With glowing hope, they stand so tall,
　The bravest blooms are here for all.
In every crack, joy finds a chance,
　In this festival, we all can dance.

Resilience Woven in Nature's Weft

In cracks of pavement, green pokes through,
A dandelion dreams of being a view.
It whispers to passersby with a grin,
"I may be a nuisance, but I thrive on a whim!"

Oh, look at that clover, with charm in its fold,
Wearing three leaves and feeling quite bold.
It calls to the bees, all buzzing and slick,
"Join me for lunch, my nectar's the trick!"

A plant in the garden, a pet of the earth,
With roots like a dancer, it knows its worth.
It waves to the wind, a kaleidoscope mess,
"I may be chaotic, but I'm truly blessed!"

So let's raise a toast to what grows in the cracks,
For even in disarray, there is no lack.
With chuckles of laughter, let nature play on,
In the tapestry wild, a bright marigold dawn.

Abundance in the Wilds

Out in the meadow where the daisies dance,
A squirrel steals seeds, oh what a chance!
It leaps with a jig, as if on parade,
Who knew that a nut could add to the charade?

The thistle wears purple, a crown on its head,
With a prickly demeanor, it's well overhead.
"Come take a selfie, but mind the sharp end,
I'm fierce and I'm funny, your garden's best friend!"

The wild onions laugh with a pungent delight,
Saying, "I'm in pasta, and oh, what a sight!
While lilies just pout, I'm making a scene,
A flavor explosion, if you know what I mean!"

So wander through wilds with a grin and a cheer,
For nature's a jester, with antics so clear.
With petals and roots, it's a fancy affair,
Abundance awaits, so step lightly with care!

Life's Unapologetic Flourish

In cracks and crevices, a bold sprout appears,
Shouting, "Hey world, I've discarded my fears!"
With colors so bright, it waves to the sky,
"Who needs a schedule? I'm here just to fly!"

A rogue cucumber rolls with a grin so wide,
"My vine is my anchor, I'm full of pride!
I may be a veggie, but watch me perform,
The salad's not ready until I've transformed!"

And here comes the morning glories, so spry,
Twisting their tendrils, trying to fly.
"Watch us as we bloom, we're the life of the show,
Unapologetic, we're always in tow!"

So gather ye wildlings, with joy in your heart,
For life's a circus, we all play a part.
In every ditch, let the laughter unfurl,
At this wild party, come dance and twirl!

Nature's Delightful Disarray

In gardens of chaos, a riot unfolds,
With tangles of color and stories retold.
A ladybug winks, with spots so divine,
"I'm lost in this mess, but darling, I shine!"

The grasshoppers leap, with a boisterous cheer,
Playing hopscotch on patches, drawing near.
"Life's not so simple, let's flip and let fly,
In this carnival of green, come laugh as we try!"

Petunias giggle, their petals askew,
Dancing in sync with the warm summer dew.
"Disarray is our art, a whimsical spree,
Join in the chaos, come sing along free!"

So here's to the wild, unfettered yet bright,
With nature's own humor, what a splendid sight!
From messy to merry, let's all have our say,
In this delightful chaos, we laugh and we play!

Hidden Gardens of the Overlooked

In cracks and corners, life does sprout,
With every poke, they dance about.
A dandelion wears a golden crown,
While bold clovers laugh, never a frown.

Beneath the fence where no one sees,
A little patch of bright green tease.
They wave their hands, so wild and free,
Claiming a space, oh let them be!

A bustling crew of misfit leaves,
They plot and plan, oh what a weave!
With secret meetings and giggles galore,
Dancing in chaos, always wanting more.

So here's to the gardens we often miss,
With every sprig, let's make a wish.
For in the odd, there's beauty untold,
In laughter, warmth, like sunshine's gold.

Resilience in the Shadows

In the darkest nooks, where laughter's shy,
They peek out shyly, oh me, oh my!
With roots entwined like gossiping friends,
They laugh at storms, for their spirit never bends.

A mismatched crew of the bold and the slight,
Try to take flight, in leftover light.
With a poke and a prod, they stand proud and tall,
Braving the odds, they'll never fall.

Thorns whisper secrets to those who'll hear,
While flowers giggle, devoid of fear.
In hidden corners with grand ambitions,
They plot their path, with no inhibitions.

Though grimy and grunge might tend to define,
With wild abandon, they sip on sunshine.
So raise a glass, to the odd and the weird,
For life's in the struggle, and we've all cheered!

Whimsical Growth Along the Path

On the sidewalk cracked, they wiggle with glee,
In vibrant hues, they shout, "Look at me!"
Hot pinks and greens reach toward the sky,
Hoping for joy as the people stroll by.

They giggle at squirrels, and flirt with the bees,
Create pirouettes in the warm summer breeze.
A raucous affair of petals and stems,
They plot their mischief like cheeky little gems.

Chasing the raindrops like little elf sprites,
They sprout in delight when the sun finally bites.
In shades of chaos, they bloom without care,
Making the mundane feel rare and quite fair.

So let's cheer for the blunders, the growth out of line,
For every odd twist is potentially fine.
In a world of perfection, what joy it can bring,
When whimsical growth sings as we dance and we swing.

Affection from the Mistakes of Nature

In every error that nature can show,
Resilience blooms from the seeds that we sow.
A patch of wildness, a tangled affair,
Where hopes and blunders mix light with despair.

Tangled tendrils with no sense of grace,
Yet they gather the sun with a jubilant face.
In messy bouquets, their charm stays intact,
Like a surprise party, you never quite fact.

Pineapples sprout where tomatoes once grew,
Unexpected guests in the garden's great brew.
They wave their arms, like they're leading a band,
With smiles and laughter, they always withstand.

So here's to the darlings, the snafus divine,
Each topsy-turvy twist is simply just fine.
For in nature's laughter, so wild and so free,
We find joy in mess, in love's jubilee!

Threads of Magic in the Wilderness

In the garden, things go wild,
A broccoli dressed like a child,
Carrots dance in their orange suits,
While radishes play peekaboo roots.

Lettuce whispers all the news,
Underneath the yellowed hues,
Tomatoes throw a little sass,
While beans climb high and just surpass.

Dandelions wear crowns of gold,
While zucchinis are really bold,
Every patch has tales to tell,
In a kingdom where plants rebel.

So join the fun in this green space,
Where veggies twirl in a lively race,
A party grows beneath the sun,
In this realm, let laughter run.

Flourish in the Fringe

Out in the edges, growth is sly,
With weeds that wave and seldom lie,
Petunias swap their flowery tricks,
While violets narrate their picnics.

Chives will giggle, quite the prank,
As radishes don their bright colored tank,
Lavender scents the air with glee,
While snails compete in a slow spree.

Tiny sprouts in a play of hide,
Grow tall and proud with some plant pride,
Little ones juggle seeds from afar,
As pumpkins aspire to be a star.

With every gust, they dance and sway,
Fringe dwellers cheer for another day,
Nature's jesters, loud and free,
In thriving chaos, joy we see.

Hues of the Uncultivated

Brushstrokes wild on nature's canvas,
Colors spill where no one planned this,
Sunflowers wear smiles, big and bright,
While thistles join in a playful fight.

Chickweed's plotting a bold coup,
While clover plays games with morning dew,
Poppies giggle in fields of dreams,
With petals flapping like silly themes.

An unwelcome guest? Not at all,
They throw parties and have a ball,
In tangled lawns of every hue,
The grace of chaos shines right through.

Laugh with the greens that skip and prance,
In this artful, spontaneous dance,
Unruly blooms that twist and bend,
In vibrant mischief, joy won't end.

Echoes of Vibrant Divergence

In the nooks, oddities thrive,
With snappy greens that come alive,
Bursts of color, a sight to see,
Nature's own patchwork jubilee.

Funky sprouts strike a quirky pose,
While lilacs gossip, goodness knows,
But thorns don't mind, they're part of the game,
All join in, no one's to blame.

Every leaf has a quirky tale,
In tangled realms where joys prevail,
Bramble bushes hum a tune,
Underneath the laughing moon.

With every whim, they spin and roll,
Bringing laughter, feeding the soul,
So join the chorus, let it ring,
In nature's dance, we're all the king.

www.ingramcontent.com/pod-product-compliance
Lightning Source LLC
Chambersburg PA
CBHW051635160426
43209CB00004B/653